SCIENCE ESSENTIALS

ASTRONOMY AND SPACE

GOING BEYOND THE GALAXY
THERE IS VAST SPACE THAT WE CAN SEE
THE TWINKLING STARS SHINING BRIGHT
I WONDER WHAT'S THERE BEYOND THAT LIGHT

THE EIGHT PLANETS AROUND THE SUN
EXPLORING COMETS AND METEORS WOULD BE FUN
SOLAR FLARES, BLACK HOLES AND THE BIG BANG
ASTEROIDS, DWARF PLANETS, AND THE MILKY WAY TRAIL
ARE LIKE MYSTERIES TO BE EXPLAINED

ROCKETS, SHUTTLES AND SPACE STATIONS
TAKE ASTRONAUTS LONG WAY THROUGH SPACE
AND HELP THEM LEARN FACTS
TO BRING BACK TO BASE.

DAD, IT'S SO FASCINATING TO LOOK AT THE STARS. I WANT TO FLY UP THERE AND EXPLORE THE SPACE.
FOR THAT YOU NEED TO STUDY ASTRONOMY AND BECOME AN ASTRONAUT.

DAD, WHAT DOES IT TAKES TO BE AN ASTRONAUT?
YOU NEED TO STUDY A LOT BEFORE THAT. LET'S GET STARTED BY LEARNING ABOUT SPACE AND ASTRONOMY.

WHAT IS SPACE?
EVERYTHING IN THE UNIVERSE BEYOND EARTH'S ATMOSPHERE IS SPACE. IT IS VAST AND SILENT.
WHAT IS THERE IN SPACE?
COMET
URANUS
VENUS
MARS
NEPTUNE
MERCURY
SUN
EARTH
SATURN
JUPITER
THE SUN, MOON, STARS, PLANETS, GALAXIES, BLACK HOLES, CLOUDS OF GAS AND DUST ARE ALL PART OF SPACE.
WHAT DOESN'T SPACE HAVE?
A PLACE WITHOUT AIR IS CALLED VACUUM. WE CANNOT HEAR ANYTHING IN VACUUM BECAUSE SOUND CANNOT TRAVEL THROUGH IT.
SPACE DOESN'T HAVE AIR AND WATER. THERE'S NO SOUND EITHER.

WHY IS SPACE DARK?

SPACE HAS NOTHING TO REFLECT LIGHT SO IT IS DARK. IF WE LOOK AT THE EARTH FROM SPACE, IT LOOKS LIT UP BECAUSE IT REFLECTS THE LIGHT FROM THE SUN.

WHERE DOES SPACE BEGIN?

WE CAN SAY THAT THE SPACE BEGINS OUTSIDE THE EARTH'S ATMOSPHERE, WHERE THERE IS NO AIR. OUR ATMOSPHERE GRADUALLY FADES INTO SPACE.

WHERE DOES SPACE END?

SCIENTISTS BELIEVE THAT THERE IS NO END TO SPACE. IF WE TRAVEL TO SPACE WE WOULD KEEP TRAVELING INTO INFINITE.

EARLY IDEAS OF SPACE

THERE WERE MANY THEORIES RELATED TO THE EARTH IN EARLIER TIMES. SOME OF THE MOST POPULAR ONES WERE:

EARTH-CENTRED UNIVERSE

IN THE ANCIENT TIMES, PEOPLE BELIEVED THAT THE EARTH WAS AT THE CENTER OF THE UNIVERSE, AND THE SUN, THE MOON AND THE STARS REVOLVED AROUND IT.

THE THEORY THAT THE EARTH WAS AT THE CENTER OF THE UNIVERSE IS CALLED GEOCENTRIC THEORY.

IT WAS POLISH ASTRONOMER, NICOLAUS COPERNICUS, WHO STATED THAT THE SUN WAS AT THE CENTER OF THE SOLAR SYSTEM. BUT HIS THEORIES WERE NOT ACCEPTED.

FLAT EARTH
LONG AGO, PEOPLE BELIEVED THAT THE EARTH WAS FLAT. IF THEY WENT TOO FAR, THEY WOULD FALL OFF THE EDGE!
IN 1519, FERDINAND MAGELLAN SET SAIL FROM SPAIN TO FIND A WESTERN ROUTE TO THE MOLUCCAS. THOUGH HE COULD NOT REACH HIS DESTINATION, ONE OF HIS SHIPS RETURNED TO SPAIN AFTER CIRCUMNAVIGATING THE EARTH. THIS PROVED THAT THE EARTH WAS ROUND.

CIRCULAR ORBITS

PEOPLE IN OLDEN DAYS THOUGHT THAT THE PLANETS REVOLVED IN CIRCULAR ORBITS. BUT...

...THEIR CALCULATIONS DID NOT MATCH THE MOVEMENT OF THE CELESTIAL OBJECTS.

IN 1609, GERMAN MATHEMATICIAN JOHANNES KEPLER FOUND THAT THE PLANETS MOVED IN ELLIPTICAL ORBITS.

WHAT AN ACHIEVEMENT!

THE GREEK ASTRONOMER HIPPARCHUS IS CONSIDERED THE GREATEST SCIENTIST OF ANTIQUITY. HE DISCOVERED:

- THAT THE EARTH ROTATES ON A TILTED AXIS, WHICH CAUSED SEASONS.
- THAT THE MOON HAD AN ELLIPTICAL ORBIT AND THAT ITS SPEED VARIES.
- THE DISTANCE FROM EARTH TO THE MOON BY COMPARING A SOLAR ECLIPSE.

HE CATEGORIZED ALL THE STARS IN ORDER OF THEIR BRIGHTNESS AND PLOTTED THEIR POSITIONS IN THE SKY ON THE FIRST STAR CHART.

TELESCOPE
THE TURNING POINT

AROUND 400 YEARS AGO, A SPECIAL TOOL CALLED THE TELESCOPE WAS INVENTED. IT PROVED NICOLAUS COPERNICUS HAD BEEN RIGHT THAT THE SUN WAS THE CENTER OF THE SOLAR SYSTEM.

YEAR 1608

DUTCH EYEGLASS MAKER HANS LIPPERSHEY DISCOVERED THAT FARAWAY OBJECTS LOOKED LARGER WHEN TWO LENSES WERE FITTED IN A LONG TUBE. THIS IS HOW THE TELESCOPE WAS BORN.

A TELESCOPE IS AN INSTRUMENT THAT HELPS US OBSERVE DISTANT OBJECTS. IT MAKES THESE OBJECTS LOOK LARGER.

YEAR 1609

ITALIAN ASTRONOMER GALILEO GALILEI IMPROVED LIPPERSHEY'S TELESCOPE.

GALILEO DISCOVERED:

- MOONS OF JUPITER
- PHASES OF VENUS
- MOUNTAINS ON MOON

JUPITER

MOONS OF JUPITER

IO EUROPA GANYMEDE CALLISTO

YEAR 1668

ENGLISH SCIENTIST ISAAC NEWTON MADE THE REFLECTING TELESCOPE BY USING MIRRORS RATHER THAN LENSES. HE ALSO USED A SHORTER TUBE.

TELESCOPES TODAY
TODAY, ASTRONOMERS USE OPTICAL AND RADIO TELESCOPES TO STUDY SPACE AND CELESTIAL OBJECTS.
RADIO TELESCOPE
A RADIO TELESCOPE IS DESIGNED TO RECEIVE RADIO WAVES FROM SPACE. IT HAS AN ANTENNA, A RECEIVER AMPLIFIER AND A RECORDER.
OPTICAL TELESCOPE
AN OPTICAL TELESCOPE USES A LENS OR MIRROR. IT GATHERS MORE LIGHT THAN THE HUMAN EYE. LARGE TELESCOPES USE MIRRORS—THE LARGER THE MIRROR, THE MORE IT CAN SEE.

THE HUBBLE SPACE TELESCOPE

THE HUBBLE SPACE TELESCOPE IS THE FIRST SPACE-BASED OPTICAL TELESCOPE. IT ORBITS THE EARTH AND TAKES PICTURES OF STARS, PLANETS AND GALAXIES THAT ARE MILLIONS OF MILES AWAY FROM THE EARTH. IT IS OPERATED FROM EARTH.

HUBBLE IS 13.3 METERS (43.5 FEET) LONG – THE LENGTH OF A LARGE SCHOOL BUS.

AN AMAZING THING ABOUT THE HUBBLE TELESCOPE IS THAT IT CAN BE REPAIRED. ASTRONOMERS CAN REPLACE ITS WORN-OUT PARTS. THEY CAN ALSO FIT NEW AND ADVANCED EQUIPMENTS AND PUT THE TELESCOPE BACK IN HIGHER ORBIT.

HUBBLE IS NAMED AFTER AMERICAN ASTRONOMER EDWIN HUBBLE.

WHERE ARE WE IN SPACE?

WE LIVE ON PLANET EARTH. HAVE YOU EVER WONDERED WHERE EXACTLY DOES THE EARTH BELONG IN SPACE?

WELL, EARTH IS A PART OF THE SOLAR SYSTEM. OUR SOLAR SYSTEM IS LOCATED IN A GALAXY CALLED THE MILKY WAY.

THE MILKY WAY IS LOCATED IN A CLUSTER KNOWN AS THE LOCAL GROUP. MILLIONS OF CLUSTERS OF GALAXIES MAKE UP THE UNIVERSE.

WHAT IS THE UNIVERSE?

EVERYTHING THAT EXISTS AROUND US IS UNIVERSE. IT INCLUDES MATTER, ENERGY, SPACE, THE SOLAR SYSTEM, THE GALAXIES, STARS, EVEN YOU AND ME! MOST OF THE UNIVERSE IS MADE OF MYSTERIOUS, INVISIBLE DARK MATTER AND DARK ENERGY.

HOW OLD IS THE UNIVERSE?

THE UNIVERSE IS SAID TO BE 13.8 BILLION YEARS OLD.

THE BIG BANG!

SCIENTISTS BELIEVE THAT THE "BIG BANG" WAS THE BEGINNING OF UNIVERSE. IT IS A THEORY WHICH STATES THAT THE UNIVERSE BEGAN AS A SINGLE POINT. IT THEN EXPANDED AND STRETCHED TO GROW AS IT IS RIGHT NOW—AND IT IS STILL EXPANDING!

THE SOLAR SYSTEM

THE SOLAR SYSTEM IS OUR IMMEDIATE NEIGHBORHOOD IN THE UNIVERSE. IT CONSISTS OF THE SUN, THE PLANETS, AROUND 170-180 MOONS, COMETS, A BELT OF ASTEROIDS, DUST AND GASES. ALL THESE ARE HELD TOGETHER BY THE SUN'S GRAVITY.

PLANETS

PLANETS ARE CELESTIAL BODIES THAT REVOLVE AROUND A STAR (IN OUR CASE, THE SUN) IN A FIXED ORBIT.

MERCURY, VENUS, EARTH AND MARS - INNER PLANETS.

MERCURY- THE SMALLEST PLANET

JUPITER- THE LARGEST PLANET

JUPITER, SATURN, URANUS AND NEPTUNE- OUTER PLANETS

A PLANET:

- MUST BE IN ORBIT AROUND A STAR
- MUST BE LARGE ENOUGH FOR ITS GRAVITY TO MAKE IT SPHERICAL
- ITS ORBIT MUST BE CLEAR OF OTHER OBJECTS

DWARF PLANETS

DWARF PLANETS ARE OBJECTS THAT ORBIT THE SUN. THEY ARE SMALLER THAN A PLANET. PLUTO, ERIS, HAUMEA, MAKEMAKE AND CERES ARE THE DWARF PLANETS.

THE SUN

THE SUN IS A STAR, A HUGE BALL OF HOT, GLOWING GASES. IT IS THE SOURCE OF HEAT AND LIGHT TO ALL PLANETS IN THE SOLAR SYSTEM.

HOW OLD IS THE SUN?

THE SUN IS SAID TO BE BORN AROUND 4.6 BILLION YEARS AGO.

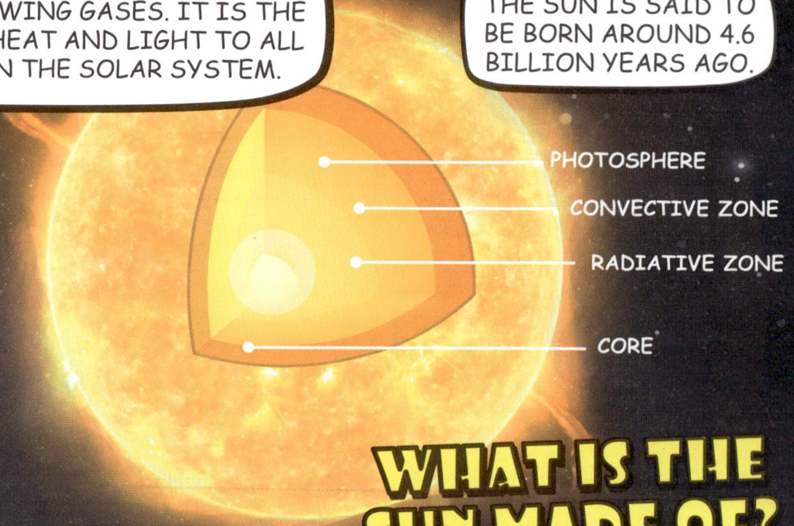

WHAT IS THE SUN MADE OF?

MOST OF THE SUN IS MADE OF HYDROGEN GAS IN PLASMA FORM. IT HAS FOUR LAYERS: CORE, RADIATIVE ZONE, CONVECTIVE ZONE AND PHOTOSPHERE.

THE SUN SPINS ON ITS AXIS JUST LIKE THE PLANETS.

SOLAR FLARE

SUDDEN BLASTS OF HOT GASES ON THE SUN'S SURFACE ARE CALLED SOLAR FLARES. THEY APPEAR IN HUGE ARCS OR LOOPS.

SUNSPOTS

SUNSPOTS ARE DARK PATCHES THAT APPEAR ON THE SUN'S SURFACE. THEY ARE COOLER THAN THE AREA AROUND THEM.

MOON

A MOON IS A NATURAL SATELLITE THAT ORBITS AROUND A PLANET AND ASTEROID. THERE ARE AROUND 181 MOONS IN THE SOLAR SYSTEM. ALL PLANETS EXCEPT MERCURY AND VENUS HAVE MOONS.

MOONS IN THE SOLAR SYSTEM

MERCURY - 0

VENUS - 0

EARTH - 1

MARS - 2

JUPITER - 80 (57 CONFIRMED, 23 PROVISIONAL)

SATURN - 83 (63 CONFIRMED, 20 PROVISIONAL)

URANUS - 27

NEPTUNE- 14

EARTH'S MOON

THE EARTH HAS ONLY ONE NATURAL SATELLITE- THE MOON. IT IS THE BRIGHTEST OBJECT IN THE NIGHT SKY. IT TAKES 27 DAYS TO ORBIT THE EARTH.

THE MOON ROTATES AROUND THE EARTH AT THE EXACT SAME SPEED AT WHICH IT REVOLVES AROUND ITS AXIS THIS IS WHY WE ONLY SEE ONE SIDE OF THE MOON.

IT HAS NO WATER OR LIFE. IT HAS NO LIGHT OF ITS OWN.

SO FAR, 12 PEOPLE HAVE WALKED ON THE MOON'S SURFACE. IT IS THE ONLY CELESTIAL BODY TO BE VISITED BY HUMANS.

IT'S SURFACE IS FULL OF CRATERS

ASTEROIDS, COMETS AND METEORS

ASTEROIDS

ASTEROIDS ARE LUMPS OF ROCK THAT ORBIT THE SUN. MOST OF THESE ARE LOCATED BETWEEN MARS AND JUPITER IN A RING-LIKE STRUCTURE CALLED THE **ASTEROID BELT**.

HALEY'S COMET IS THE MOST FAMOUS OF ALL COMETS. IT APPEARS AFTER EVERY 76 YEARS.

CERES: THE FIRST AND LARGEST ASTEROID TO BE DISCOVERED, NOW CALLED A DWARF PLANET

VESTA: THE BRIGHTEST AND SECOND LARGEST ASTEROID

COMETS

COMETS ARE BALLS OF SNOW, DUST AND ICE. THEY TOO ORBIT THE SUN.

WHEN A COMET GETS CLOSE TO THE SUN, IT WARMS UP.

THE SNOW AND ICE TURNS TO GAS FORMING TWO TAILS—DUST TAIL AND GAS TAIL.

METEORS
METEORS ARE PIECES OF DUST AND DEBRIS FROM SPACE THAT BURN UP IN THE EARTH'S ATMOSPHERE. THEY ARE VISIBLE AS BRIGHT STREAKS OF LIGHT IN THE NIGHT SKY. METEORS ARE ALSO CALLED **SHOOTING STARS**.
A METEOR THAT ENTERS THE ATMOSPHERE AND LANDS ON THE EARTH'S SURFACE IS CALLED A **METEORITE**.
WHAT A SHOWER!
EVERY YEAR, IN NOVEMBER, THE EARTH PASSES THROUGH THOUSANDS OF FRAGMENTS LEFT BEHIND BY THE TEMPEL-TUTTLE COMET.
THIS CAUSES A METEOR SHOWER CALLED THE LEONIDS IN THE NIGHT SKY. THE SHOWER IS USUALLY AT PEAK ON NOVEMBER 17 AND 18.
THE SHOWER IS CALLED LEONIDS BECAUSE IT'S RADIANT, OR THE POINT IN THE SKY WHERE THE METEORS SEEM TO EMERGE FROM, LIES IN THE CONSTELLATION LEO.

STARS

A STAR IS A HUGE BALL OF HOT GASES, MAINLY HELIUM AND HYDROGEN HELD TOGETHER BY GRAVITY. STARS ARE OF DIFFERENT TYPES—SUPERGIANT, RED GIANT, BLUE GIANT, WHITE DWARFS, ETC.

VY CANIS MAJORIS IS THE LARGEST STAR IN THE NIGHT SKY—SO LARGE THAT THE SUN CAN FIT IN AROUND 3 BILLION TIMES.

HOW DO STARS GIVE OUT LIGHT?

THE HYDROGEN ATOMS IN THE CORE OF A STAR COMBINE TO MAKE HELIUM. THIS RELEASES LARGE AMOUNTS OF HEAT AND LIGHT, MAKING THE STAR SHINE.

PROXIMA CENTAURI IS THE NEAREST STAR TO THE SUN.

CONSTELLATIONS

A CONSTELLATION IS A GROUP OF STARS THAT APPEARS TO FORM A PATTERN OR PICTURE.

THEY ARE NAMED AFTER THE MYTHICAL BEINGS THEY RESEMBLE. FOR EXAMPLE—LEO, THE LION AND ORION, THE GREAT HUNTER.

THERE ARE 88 OFFICIAL CONSTELLATIONS.

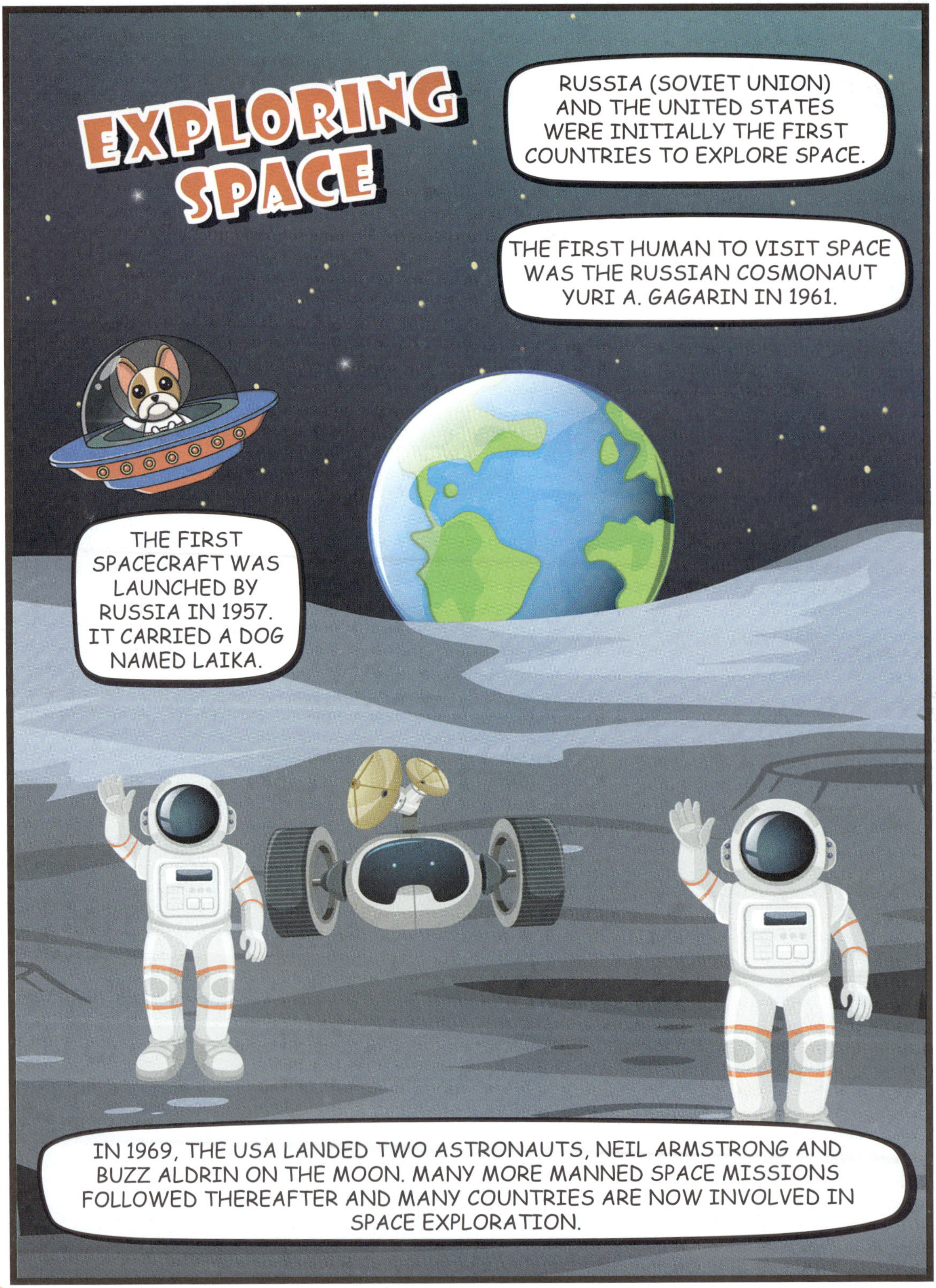
EXPLORING SPACE
RUSSIA (SOVIET UNION) AND THE UNITED STATES WERE INITIALLY THE FIRST COUNTRIES TO EXPLORE SPACE.
THE FIRST HUMAN TO VISIT SPACE WAS THE RUSSIAN COSMONAUT YURI A. GAGARIN IN 1961.
THE FIRST SPACECRAFT WAS LAUNCHED BY RUSSIA IN 1957. IT CARRIED A DOG NAMED LAIKA.
IN 1969, THE USA LANDED TWO ASTRONAUTS, NEIL ARMSTRONG AND BUZZ ALDRIN ON THE MOON. MANY MORE MANNED SPACE MISSIONS FOLLOWED THEREAFTER AND MANY COUNTRIES ARE NOW INVOLVED IN SPACE EXPLORATION.

ASTRONAUTS

ASTRONAUTS ARE PEOPLE WHO TRAVEL TO SPACE. THEY NEED HOURS OF STUDY AND RIGOROUS TRAINING TO TRAVEL TO SPACE. THEY USE REAL AIRCRAFT, SIMULATORS, VIRTUAL REALITY SYSTEMS, SPECIAL WATER TANKS TO TRAIN FOR SPACE.

AN ASTRONAUT'S SUIT

ASTRONAUTS WEAR SPECIAL SUITS TO TRAVEL TO SPACE.

DURING LAUNCH, THEY WEAR AN ORANGE COLOR **LAUNCH ENTRY SUIT** WITH HUGE POCKETS ON THE LEGS TO STORE TOOLS.

FOR A SPACEWALK, ASTRONAUTS WEAR AN **EXTRAVEHICULAR MOBILITY UNIT** (EMU). THEY HAVE ALL THE ESSENTIAL THINGS ASTRONAUTS NEED TO SURVIVE OUTSIDE THE SPACECRAFT.

TO GET TRAINING ON WEIGHTLESSNESS, ASTRONAUTS ARE PUT IN SPECIAL AIRPLANES WITH NO SEATS AND PADDED WALLS. THEY ARE CALLED 'VOMIT COMET'

ROCKETS

ROCKETS ARE VEHICLES USED TO LAUNCH A SPACECRAFT INTO SPACE BY BURNING FUEL THAT CREATES A STRONG THRUST.

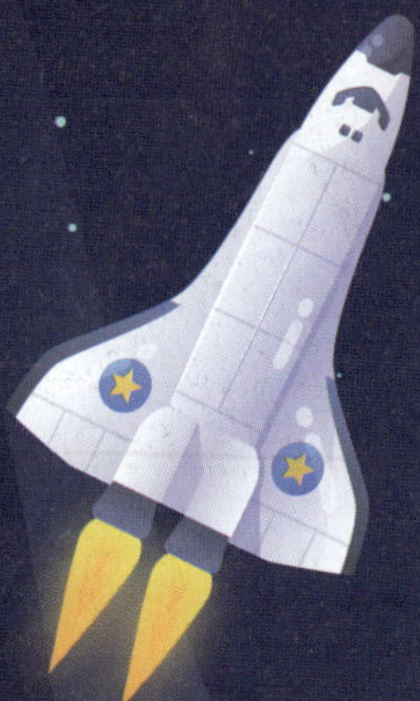

SPACE SHUTTLE

THE SPACE SHUTTLE WAS THE FIRST REUSABLE SPACECRAFT. IT WAS LAUNCHED BY NASA IN 1981 AND CARRIED OUT MORE THAN 130 SPACE MISSIONS.

IT CARRIED ASTRONAUTS AND EQUIPMENTS TO SPACE. IT NOT ONLY LAUNCHED SATELLITES BUT ALSO BUILT SPACE STATION.

SPACE STATION

A SPACE STATION IS A SPACE LAB THAT ORBITS THE EARTH. IT IS OPERATED BY ASTRONAUTS WHO STAY FOR SEVERAL WEEKS OR MONTHS ON IT.

THE FIRST SPACE STATION WAS LAUNCHED IN 1971. IT WAS CALLED SALYUT 1. SINCE THEN 12 SPACE STATIONS HAVE BEEN PLACED INTO THE EARTH'S ORBIT.

AS OF 2022, TWO FULLY ACTIVE SPACE STATIONS ORBIT THE EARTH—THE INTERNATIONAL SPACE STATION AND CHINA'S TIANGONG SPACE STATION. THESE HELP ASTRONAUTS CONTINUE THEIR JOURNEY OF EXPLORING SPACE.